SUPER SUNDAY

The Inside Slant on the Ultimate Game

SUPER SUNDAY

The Inside Slant on the Ultimate Game

Published by

Beckett Publications

15850 Dallas Parkway

Dallas, TX 75248

ISBN: 1-887432-52-3

Super Sunday is not licensed, authorized or endorsed
by any league, player or players association.

First Edition: November 1998

Corporate Sales and Information (972) 991-6657

BECKETT

FOREWORD

By Brett Favre / Packers Quarterback

I first started watching the Super Bowl as far back as I can remember. Whenever that was, I don't know — probably when I was a kid — but it was always as big of an occasion as it is today. We'd always cook out and watch the Super Bowl.

I can pretty much remember most of them in bits

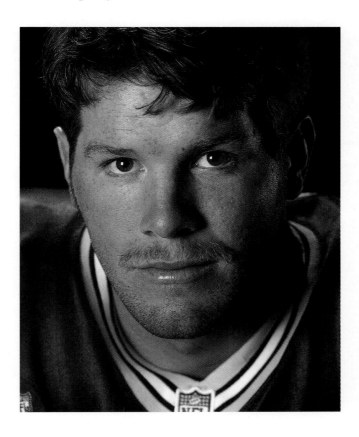

and pieces. I was a Cowboys fan growing up and I hated the Steelers, so I remember a lot of the Cowboys-Steelers rivalries. But I remember a number of the games.

I knew that is where I wanted to be someday . . . to be a football player and play in the Super Bowl.

My dream became a reality in Super Bowl XXXI (as Favre's Packers defeated the Patriots, 35-21). I felt that once I got there, I would feel like I was relieved because I had finally gotten there. But now I'm more driven to go back because it's everything I thought it would be and then some.

The bad thing is, if you lose one, it's really frustrating because you work, heck, all your life to get there, really. And, because, (for us) the one that you win is kind of brushed aside.

As we broke out the film of Super Bowl XXXII (the Broncos' 31-24 upset of the Packers) last off-season, it was kind of frustrating (to watch) knowing we could have done better. We could have won that ball game easily. If we got beat 50-0 it would be easier to swallow than the way we lost it.

I just want to go back.

CONTENTS

Louisiana Superdome, host to five Super Bowls

First Quarter

THE ULTIMATE GAME

1

MEMORABLE MOMENTS

By Dick Enberg / NBC Play-by-Play Man

It's very difficult to say which Super Bowl was the best. But I suspect you could talk me into saying XXXII was the most special and the most memorable game I ever broadcasted.

I will look back on it, my last game after 32 years of being associated with broadcasting NFL football, with a special fondness. It was already going to be a big deal, with the game in (hometown) San

TICKET TO RIDE Harley Davidson aficionado Mike Holmgren took the ride of his coaching career following the Packers' triumph over New England in Super Bowl XXXI. The victory marked the return to the throne for the NFL's smallest and proudest town, Green Bay, Wisc.

Diego, and no matter how many times you are at a Super Bowl, it's special.

And this time we had learned this would be the last game that we as a network, NBC, were to broadcast. Our contract was up.

I don't know exactly what we did in the booth when the game was over. I

TALK ISN'T CHEAP Broadway Joe Namath held court before Super Bowl III and made one of the boldest predictions in sports history, "guaranteeing" victory against the Colts, an 18-point favorite, and then pulling off the upset with an MVP performance.

LAST HURRAH Claiming five NFL titles in seven seasons deserves a fitting sendoff. Vince Lombardi, who's name adorns the Super Bowl trophy, was carried off into the sunset after Green Bay rocked the Raiders in Super Bowl II.

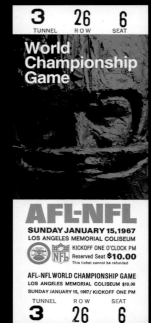

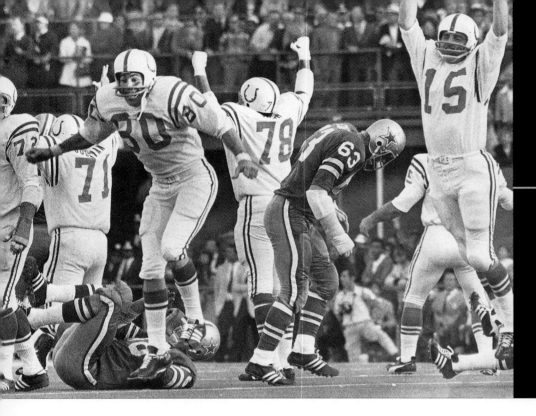

ECSTASY AND AGONY Forever frozen in time are Jim O'Brien's 32-yard field goal with five ticks left to doom Dallas in Super Bowl V, and Scott Norwood's last-second boot that veered wide right, giving the N.Y. Giants a 20-19 victory in Super Bowl XXV.

probably just shook hands or something with Phil Simms and Paul Maguire. I know

that during the game we made a conscious attempt not to be maudlin or emotional.

But I did break down a bit at a camera meeting we had the day before. I saw the sad

eyes of so many cameramen we have had an association with, and I lost it. The morn-

ing of the game, we were all focused on the job, though, as professionals.

I look back at what we did on our last broadcast and feel very good about what

we accomplished. Broadcasters are so often judged on how good the game is. I was

most proud of the work we had done in blowout games. The Bears-Patriots (Chicago,

46-10, in **XX**) with Merlin Olsen, the Cowboys-Bills (Dallas, 52-17, in **XXVII**) at the

Rose Bowl.

But we couldn't have asked for anything more from the Broncos and Packers.

"Don't listen when some-one tells you [that] you can't do this or that you don't know what it takes. Anything is possible. I think I showed that."
– Denver's Terrell Davis, a graduate of the same San Diego high school as Marcus Allen

AGAINST THE GRAIN Steve Young directed his 49ers to their record-setting fifth Super Bowl title in XXIX. Marcus Allen, whose 74-yard scamper sealed the deal in Super Bowl XVIII, was said to be "too small" and "too slow" to be a star.

It was particularly memorable, not because it was our last broadcast, but because of the AFC winning an exciting game. That lasting image of John Elway in mid-air (diving for a key first down). I really thought Green Bay was going to come back and tie it up. I got a little greedy there.

True, this was perceived as the finest Super Bowl. I'm not going to argue.

NBC broadcaster Dick Enberg has served as play-by-play man for eight Super Bowl games.

HOOPLA

By Michael T. Fiur / Halftime Producer

Halftime lasts 20 minutes. So for a halftime show, that's four or five minutes to get everything on the field, 10 or 12 for the show, and four or five to get off. Plus, we're coordinating 400 volunteers who rehearse for four weeks and don't get to watch the game in the stadium.

Radio City and the NFL start percolating about a year in advance. We go through two dozen bad ideas to find one

X-TRAVAGANZA A staple at eight Super Bowls, the Dallas Cowboys Cheerleaders will be forever linked to the big game, for which the pregame, halftime and postgame shows have been nothing short of spectacular.

GREATEST SHOW ON EARTH   Barnum & Bailey couldn't even have envisioned the phenomenon known as the Super Bowl halftime show. From the King of Pop, Michael Jackson, to a life-sized New Orleans' steamship, the 20-minute break in the game has become a production more complex than a Bill Walsh playbook and more expensive than a James Cameron film.

or two good ones, looking at everything from talent concepts, what's popular at the time, to the community the game will be played in and so on.

The Michael Jackson show, XXVII, was clearly the one that broke the mold. A year before, Fox had counter-programmed halftime with "In Living

WHAT'S NEXT? Who knows what's in store for Super Bowl fans. Once you've seen the Rocketeer, jazz superstar Al Hurt and the great hot-air balloon race, you've really seen it all . . . or have you?

Color" and the NFL issued a challenge: Bring the expectations of the halftime to the level of the game. Deliver a live show that's exciting to the people in the stands and a billion watching on TV.

Michael agreed to do the halftime because of his relationship with Radio City, and he was an incredible presence. We had put together a tape of his songs to sing, and he told us, "I like the songs, but with just bits and pieces of them, it sounds like a K-Tel ad. I want each song to have a beginning and an end."

So he reworked the music. And we

INFLATED GOALS At times, the pregame hype-fest gets a little too big for its own good. The field often becomes a circus stage with inflated objects — and sometimes un-inflated objects — littering the ground. Media Day, traditionally held on the Tuesday before Super Sunday, is another target-rich environment for unsuspecting players . . . and sometimes journalists. With questions such as, "If you were a tree, what kind of tree would you be?" (a question actually posed to Doug Williams before Super Bowl XXII) why would players take serious-ly this annual media barrage?

designed a concert-style stage that weighed like 12 tons, came in 22 pieces and contained lighting, sound, wind, smoke, pyrotechnics and an elevator lift. It all went off. It was a terrific show.

Michael T. Fiur, vice president of events for Radio City Productions, has helped produce five Super Bowl halftime shows.

3

WINNERS

By Pat Bowlen / Denver Broncos Owner

What I saw very early in the week from John Elway was a different air — an air of confidence. He was drawing it from the whole team.

It was a lot different in the '80s. That loss to San Francisco (55-10, XXIV) really sticks out. I can remember going into the locker room and John was about the last one in there and, well . . .

This time (in Super Bowl XXXII vs.

THIS ONE'S FOR JOHN Pat Bowlen's announcement brought goosebumps to any John Elway fan. After three failed attempts, Elway beat the Packers and Father Time to win Super Bowl XXX at the tender age of 37.

JUMPIN' FOR JOY The Cowboys and the 49ers had countless reasons to celebrate during their Super Bowl runs. Dallas' cocky young stallions twice galloped over

Francisco twice stuffed Cincinnati, rocked Marino's Dolphins and embarrassed Elway's Broncos during their '80s juggernaut. The core groups of these two squads

the Packers) the turning point to me was on our first possession, after they'd scored. We scored and I could see then that it was going to be a good game. John was so determined. When John dived into (three defenders) in the third quarter, my thought was, "Don't get hurt. Don't drop the ball." When he threw that interception, I was mad. But that's John and that incredible desire to win.

John and I have a very rare relationship; we've worked together for 14 years.

PINNACLE OF THEIR PROFESSION   Tom Landry (upper left) finally cracked a smile after winning his first Super Bowl, VI, against the Dolphins. Bill Parcells rode on the shoulders of his favorite player, Lawrence Taylor, in Super Bowl XXV. Vince Lombardi admired HIS trophy after Super Bowl I.

"They made this game for quarterbacks, and you've got to win this game to be up there with the elite. It wouldn't have been a complete career otherwise."

- John Elway,

a modest 12 of 22 for 123 yards passing in Super Bowl XXXII

That's unusual in the NFL these days, with free agency and other factors.

So after the game (a 31-24 Denver victory), I knew what I wanted to do, what I wanted to say. The game was all about John Elway – that's where the emotion was throughout the country. He'd waited so long and kept driving for this moment.

That's why I said, "This one's for John." He'd finally won the Super Bowl.

During Pat Bowlen's first 14 years as president of the Broncos, his team played in five AFC Championship Games and four Super Bowls.

LEGENDS

*By Dan Fouts / Former San Diego
Chargers Quarterback*

When I was still playing I wasn't too interested in the Super Bowl, because I never made it to one. And I, like every player on the other 26 teams who was frustrated at the end of the season, managed to avoid them.

Here's what I would do:

As you know, they play the Pro Bowl every year the week after the Super Bowl. Six times I was chosen to play in

SUPER SUB As a backup for Earl Morrall in Super Bowl III, Johnny Unitas engineered the Colts' lone scoring drive, albeit in a losing effort. Johnny U. later hit Super Bowl paydirt as a starter thanks to a rookie placekicker and a stout defensive stand.

CLASSIC COMBINATION The 49ers' dynamic duo of Joe Montana and Jerry Rice was unequalled in NFL history and always saved its best for late January. Against Denver in Super Bowl XXIV, Montana to Rice accounted for three scores, 148 yards and countless shattered nerves in the Broncos' secondary.

that game, over in Hawaii. So I'd arrange my schedule so I could take a flight during the Super Bowl, to be in the air while the game was going on. Because I didn't want to be watching with a lot of people who were having a good time, whooping it up.

So you remember the 747s that had the lounge upstairs? That's where I'd go during the Super Bowl. That's where I found refuge: at 35,000 feet upstairs, one of those drinks with the little umbrellas in it in my hand. It's the only way to spend Super Bowl Sunday. I recommend it.

Actually, I'm not one of those guys

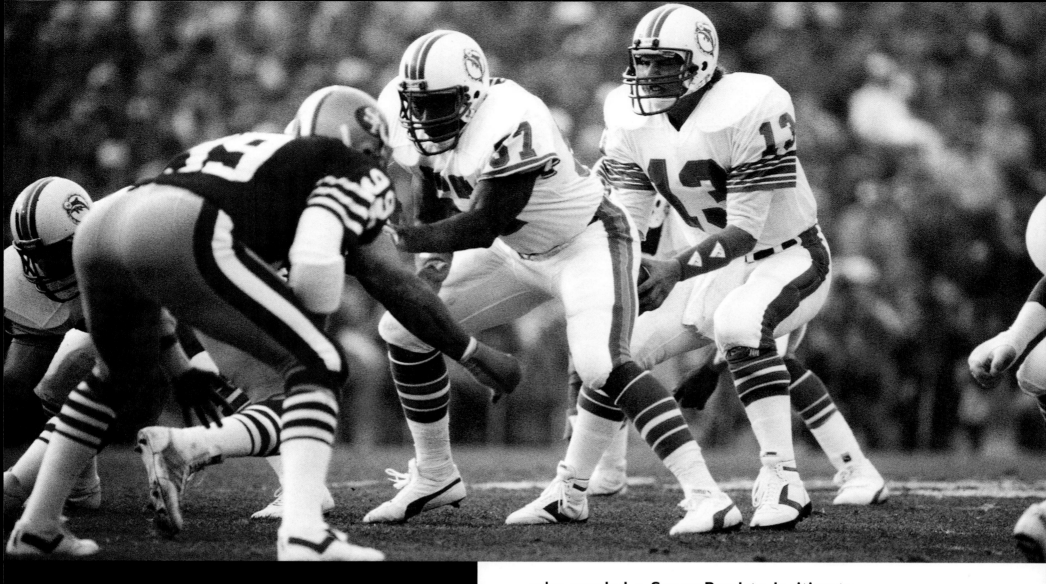

THE JAW Don Shula's cool sideline demeanor masked an emotional volcano that raged inside during the last minutes of Super Bowl VII as Shula's unbeaten Dolphins held on to a perilous seven-point lead against the Redskins. Thankfully for the winningest coach in NFL history — and his team — Miami won the game, kept its per-

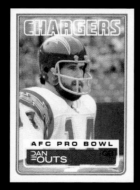

fect season intact and presented its field general with his first of two Super Bowl trophies. Still, one has to wonder how close Garo Yepremium got to Shula in the locker room after the game.

THE ARM Dan Marino's swagger and lightning-quick release reminded many of a certain brash young quarterback who made his living on Broadway. Unfortunately for the immensely talented Marino, his one ultimate journey — Super Bowl XIX against Montana's 49ers — didn't turn out as well as it had for Joe Namath.

who needed a Super Bowl to legitimate or validate my career. We had some great, exciting teams in San Diego. We gave it our best shot, I gave it my best effort, and it was rewarding enough for me to be in the Hall of Fame.

But when I did retire, I did think about the Super Bowl. The Chargers

were going in a different direction at that point. If (Don) Coryell was still the coach at that point, and said let's give it one more shot, I would've stuck around, sure, for a chance to play in that game.

As quarterback of the Chargers from 1973 to 1987, Dan Fouts passed for 43,040 yards, fifth-best in NFL history.

RUNNING MATES Arguably, these four horsemen were the premier running backs of their respective decades — Franco Harris (right) and Larry Csonka (below) ruled the '70s, while Walter Payton (upper left) and John Riggins ran wild in the '80s. They did it in similar tough-guy fashion, a combination of brute force and deft footwork. Their combined Super Bowl record of 8-2 illustrates their dominance.

"John Riggins constantly bashed the Dolphins until they finally broke in the fourth. . . . I could hear the violent collisions."

– Photographer

Tony Tomsic,

on SB XVII

Second
Quarter

DECADES OF DOMINATION

5

THE 60S

By Vern Biever / NFL Photographer

I always felt before each game started

that by simply showing up the Green Bay

Packers were seven to 10 points better

than the other teams.

It's not that the other teams were

scared of them, but it was that the

Packers could back up those numbers.

Like head coach Vince Lombardi said,

"We never lost a game; we just ran out of

time — just ran out of minutes."

UNSTOPPABLE FORCE Regardless of who took Bart Starr's handoff, the Packers' ground game steamrolled opponents behind a line named Kramer, Gregg, Thurston, Skoronski and Curry.

Starr's rewards for two MVP awards: two Vettes, and the ultimate compliment from his coach. *"He can throw with anyone,"* Lombardi said. *"I'm delighted that he's finally getting the attention he has long deserved."*

They were just so superior.

But you've got to give Lombardi credit. That whole team, they performed for him. He molded the team together. He was a very dedicated guy. He put work up on such a high level that he applied himself at all times.

He was a different type of person compared to other coaches I've pho-

tographed along the sidelines through the years.

His players stayed together and they talked together. Lombardi instilled in them a sense of togetherness, and for the most part, these guys were very successful in business after their respective careers were over. "Get along well with people, and apply yourself." I think he taught them that as well.

GOOD SEATS REMAIN   In Super Bowl I, the NFL couldn't give tickets away as more than 40,000 empty seats in the Los Angeles Coliseum greeted the Packers and Chiefs. A year later, the world champion Packers and AFL champion Oakland Raiders drew an overflow crowd at the Orange Bowl in Miami. The rest, as they say, is history.

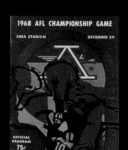

GENERATION NEXT In the first two Super Bowls, rugged-to-the-core Ray Nitschke (No. 66) and his Packers proved the dominance of the NFL by burying the upstart AFL. But when Broadway Joe Namath gunned his Jets past the Colts in Super Bowl III, and then Len Dawson's Chiefs beat the Vikings the following season, the AFL finally could look its older brother in the eye without blinking.

After a while I became second nature to these guys. If I wasn't there, they'd be surprised. As far as I know, I think I'm the only guy who got that picture of Lombardi receiving the first Super Bowl trophy (now the Lombardi Trophy) from Pete Rozelle (following Green Bay's 35-10 victory over Kansas City on the inaugural Super Sunday).

Even today I consider myself a close friend with most of them. So when one of the guys, Ray Nitschke, recently died, I went to the funeral. All the same guys were there: Bart Starr, Paul Hornung . . . It was just like old times. They were all talking, and once again it was a close-knit operation.

Vern Biever is one of just six photographers who have documented all Super Bowls.

6

THE 70S

By Jack Ham / Steelers Linebacker

One thing we had going for us was (head coach) Chuck Noll. He learned a valuable lesson as an assistant coach when he was with Don Shula and the Colts lost to the Jets in Super Bowl III.

He'd always say to us that once you make the game bigger than life, you're in trouble. The Colts? They'd say, "It's such a big game, it's not like basketball or hockey or baseball, where there's a best of

FOUR FOR FOUR Dallas and Miami made early bids to dominate the decade, but two-time MVP Terry Bradshaw and the Steelers separated themselves from the pack with four victories in six years.

seven." They made too much out of

the Super Bowl. They didn't talk to the

press too much.

Chuck took the exact opposite

approach. He treated the Super Bowl like

it was another game. We had Monday

and Tuesday off in both Miami (for X and

ART OF THE STEEL When Steelers owner Art Rooney hired Chuck Noll (left) as head coach in 1969, the team was coming off a record of 2-11-1. Then Noll quickly constructed the superstructure of a dynasty. The foundation was the Steel Curtain defense, which would produce HOFers Mel Blount, Mean Joe Greene, Jack Ham (above) and Jack Lambert.

NO PLACE LIKE HOME Two weeks after winning their first conference title in 42 years, the Steelers claimed their first world title in Super Bowl IX, as tackle Ernie Holmes and the rest of the defense held Minnesota to an unheard of 17 yards rushing.

XIII) and New Orleans (for IX). In fact, when we were in New Orleans, Andy Russell and Ray Mansfield ended up losing a rental car because we were out so late. Hey, they were the elder statesmen on the team. Setting Ray loose on Bourbon Street is a scary thought.

But I think our guys were pretty mature players. We knew what we could or couldn't do. There was no curfew on Monday, Tuesday or Wednesday of Super Bowl week, and we enjoyed ourselves.

PERFECTION PLUS After watching his Dolphins fall to Dallas in Super Bowl VI, Don Shula drove his team to back-to-back world titles: perfection in 1972 and two losses in '73, culminated by Larry Csonka's 145-yard demolition of the Vikings in Super Bowl VIII.

BACK IN THE SADDLE Two Super Bowl rings in the '70s failed to soothe the sting of defeat for Tom Landry and his Cowboys, who missed grabbing three more rings by a grand total of 11 points.

Chuck would say, "You don't have to stay in your room." And, "Don't make the game bigger than it is." I think some of the younger players were shocked by the approach he was taking.

Chuck even would downplay the whole media thing. He'd tell us to talk to the press, tell stories, have some fun. Heck, any time you put a microphone in front of Ray or Andy, they can do a 20-minute stand-up routine.

But we had fun. And it paid off.

Hall of Fame linebacker Jack Ham was a member of all four Pittsburgh championship teams, but didn't play in Super Bowl XIV because of an ankle injury.

7

THE 80S

By Randy Cross / Former 49ers Center

I'm probably a little prejudiced, but I think the best team the 49ers ever had was in 1984. It's not just because that team had the best record of the five (15-1 in the regular season, 18-1 overall), but a lot of key players were at their peaks, and we sort of steamrolled people.

I think the area that made that team the best was defense. People overlook defense fairly glaringly when they talk

NO BRAG, JUST FACT   Joe Montana's Super Bowl stat sheet says it all about the Quarterback and Team of the Decade: 4-for-4 on Super Sunday, and career records for MVP awards (three), passing yards (1,142) and touchdown passes (11).

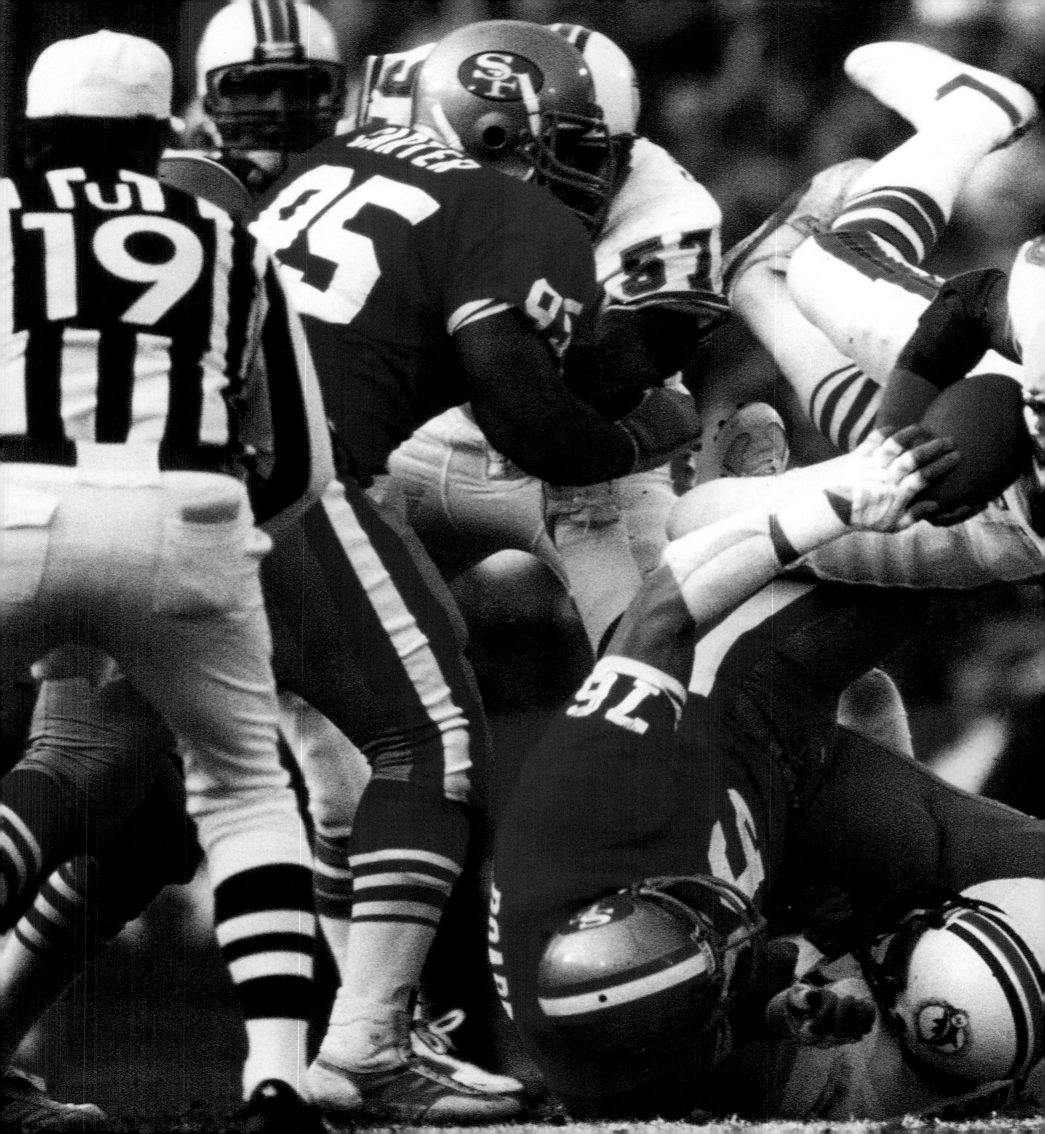

CASE FOR THE DEFENSE   The 49ers' edged Cincinnati, 26-21, in XVI for victory No. 1 of the decade, and their return engagement three years later vs. Miami was expected to be close, too. Miami boasted Dangerous Dan Marino and his record-smashing 48 touchdown passes in the 1984 season. So much for hype. The 49ers defense grounded Marino and Co., and Montana was flawless, completing 24 of 35 passes for 331 yards and three TDs.

HOME SWEET HOME Playing Miami at Stanford Stadium, the 49ers felt at home — and played like it. Guard Randy Cross (51) and his linemates helped the offense roll up 537 total yards to the Dolphins' 314.

DA BEARS The 1985 season belonged to Chicago. Led by Walter Payton, the "46" defense and the antics of Jim McMahon and Refrigerator Perry, the Bears humiliated New England in Super Bowl XX.

about the 49er teams. The defensive personnel on that '84 team was incredible: Fred Dean, Gary Johnson, Louie Kelcher, Manu Tuiasosopo and Lawrence Pillers up front, Jack Reynolds and Keena Turner at linebacker, Ronnie Lott, Eric Wright, Carlton Williamson and Dwight Hicks in the secondary. That's what made us so dominant. It's easy to play offense when you have such a good defense, because it puts so much pressure on the other team, every single possession.

"*The '81 team was young and naïve. The '84 club was confident. The '88 team was on the ropes all the time. [The '89] team could focus on the matter at hand.*"

— 49ers linebacker Keena Turner summarizing a dynasty

Our defensive schemes were really good. George Seifert was defensive coordinator, and he was an absolute master at using personnel. Situation substitution was always thought of as kind of an offensive thing, but he used it on defense. And he had blitz packages that I think all 11 guys were in. He had so much faith in everybody.

Randy Cross, a three-time Pro Bowl guard and center, played on the 49ers' first three Super Bowl squads.

SECOND BEST If not for San Francisco, the Washington Redskins could lay claim to the 1980s. Joe Gibbs' squads celebrated victories over Miami (XVII) and Denver (XXII), and fell to Oakland (XVIII).

THE 90S

By Jimmy Johnson / Former Dallas Cowboys Head Coach

We felt like in the first Super Bowl (a 52-17 rout by Dallas in XXVII) we had an advantage over Buffalo in that they were a very talented team, but they were using their great defense to overcome turnovers by their offense.

(That's why) when we beat San Francisco (in the NFC title game), we believed we were home free. We thought Buffalo would turn it over, and we were

RING OF FIRE Ignited by an arsenal of offensive weapons such as Troy Aikman, Emmitt Smith, Daryl "Moose" Johnston, Michael Irvin, Alvin Harper and Jay Novacek, the Cowboys rang up 82 points on the Bill's in back-to-back Super Bowls.

not a team that would turn it over. In

fact, that particular year we had only one

interception and no fumbles in the play-

offs up until Leon Lett fumbled (against

Buffalo) after we had scored 52 points.

So, I knew we weren't going to turn it

over and Buffalo was. I told the players

the night before we were going to be

PRAISING ARIZONA   The world's biggest game arrived in Arizona in 1996. The Cowboys outlasted the Steelers, 27-17, in Super Bowl XXX held at Sun Devil Stadium in Tempe.

FOUR BY FOUR   Thurman Thomas and the Bills dominated the AFC in the '90s, winning four straight conference championships, but never grasped a Super Bowl victor's ring.

GIFTED   Jimmy Johnson predicted that the Bills' mistake-prone offense would provide Dallas plenty of scoring opportunities in Super Bowl XXVII. Defensive tackle Jimmie Jones returned one Bills fumble for a touchdown.

CAN'T CATCH 22 Emmitt Smith's 10-yard burst against the Bills in Super Bowl XXVII became the first of a record five career Super Bowl rushing touchdowns.

really conservative early in the game. We were going to run the ball, be conservative with blitzes, and once Buffalo turned it over, then we would open it up.

So I told them not to get frustrated. . . . and sure enough, the turnovers started coming. We got the (Jim) Kelly interception, then we got the fumble and (defensive tackle) Jimmie Jones got the touchdown. It was one right after another. I think we got nine. It kind of played out like what we had planned.

In three years, Cowboys head coach Jimmy Johnson turned a 1-15 team into a world champion, not once but twice.

ALL-TIME RESULTS

Game	Date	Result	Site	MVP
I	Jan. 15, 1967	Green Bay 35, Kansas City 10	Memorial Coliseum, Los Angeles	Bart Starr, QB, Green Bay
II	Jan. 14, 1968	Green Bay 33, Oakland 14	Orange Bowl, Miami	Bart Starr, QB, Green Bay
III	Jan. 12, 1969	N.Y. Jets 16, Baltimore 7	Orange Bowl, Miami	Joe Namath, QB, Jets
IV	Jan. 11, 1970	Kansas City 23, Minnesota 7	Tulane Stadium, New Orleans	Len Dawson, QB, Kansas City
V	Jan. 17, 1971	Baltimore 16, Dallas 13	Orange Bowl, Miami	Chuck Howley, LB, Dallas
VI	Jan. 16, 1972	Dallas 24, Miami 3	Tulane Stadium, New Orleans	Roger Staubach, QB, Dallas
VII	Jan. 14, 1973	Miami 14, Washington 7	Memorial Coliseum, Los Angeles	Jake Scott, S, Miami
VIII	Jan. 13, 1974	Miami 24, Minnesota 7	Rice Stadium, Houston	Larry Csonka, FB, Miami
IX	Jan. 12, 1975	Pittsburgh 16, Minnesota 6	Tulane Stadium, New Orleans	Franco Harris, RB, Pittsburgh
X	Jan. 18, 1976	Pittsburgh 21, Dallas 17	Orange Bowl, Miami	Lynn Swann, WR, Pittsburgh
XI	Jan. 9, 1977	Oakland 32, Minnesota 14	Rose Bowl, Pasadena	Fred Biletnikoff, WR, Oakland
XII	Jan. 15, 1978	Dallas 27, Denver 10	Superdome, New Orleans	Harvey Martin, DE, Randy White, DT, Dallas
XIII	Jan. 21, 1979	Pittsburgh 35, Dallas 31	Orange Bowl, Miami	Terry Bradshaw, QB, Pittsburgh
XIV	Jan. 20, 1980	Pittsburgh 31, Los Angeles 19	Rose Bowl, Pasadena	Terry Bradshaw, QB, Pittsburgh
XV	Jan. 25, 1981	Oakland 27, Philadelphia 10	Superdome, New Orleans	Jim Plunkett, QB, Oakland
XVI	Jan. 24, 1982	San Francisco 26, Cincinnati 21	Silverdome, Pontiac, Mich.	Joe Montana, QB, San Francisco
XVII	Jan. 30, 1983	Washington 27, Miami 17	Rose Bowl, Pasadena	John Riggins, RB, Washington
XVIII	Jan. 22, 1984	L.A. Raiders 38, Washington 9	Tampa Stadium, Tampa	Marcus Allen, RB, Raiders
XIX	Jan. 20, 1985	San Francisco 38, Miami 16	Stanford Stadium, Stanford	Joe Montana, QB, San Francisco
XX	Jan. 26, 1986	Chicago 46, New England 10	Superdome, New Orleans	Richard Dent, DE, Chicago
XXI	Jan. 25, 1987	N.Y. Giants 39, Denver 20	Rose Bowl, Pasadena	Phil Simms, QB, Giants
XXII	Jan. 31, 1988	Washington 42, Denver 10	Jack Murphy Stadium, San Diego	Doug Williams, QB, Washington
XXIII	Jan. 22, 1989	San Francisco 20, Cincinnati 16	Joe Robbie Stadium, Miami	Jerry Rice, WR, San Francisco
XXIV	Jan. 28, 1990	San Francisco 55, Denver 10	Superdome, New Orleans	Joe Montana, QB, San Francisco
XXV	Jan. 27, 1991	N.Y. Giants 20, Buffalo 19	Tampa Stadium, Tampa	Ottis Anderson, RB, Giants
XXVI	Jan. 26, 1992	Washington 37, Buffalo 24	Metrodome, Minneapolis	Mark Rypien, QB, Washington
XXVII	Jan. 31, 1993	Dallas 52, Buffalo 17	Rose Bowl, Pasadena	Troy Aikman, QB, Dallas
XXVIII	Jan. 30, 1994	Dallas 30, Buffalo 13	Georgia Dome, Atlanta	Emmitt Smith, RB, Dallas
XXIX	Jan. 29, 1995	San Francisco 49, San Diego 26	Joe Robbie Stadium, Miami	Steve Young, QB, San Francisco
XXX	Jan. 28, 1996	Dallas 27, Pittsburgh 17	Sun Devil Stadium, Tempe	Larry Brown, CB, Dallas
XXXI	Jan. 26, 1997	Green Bay 35, New England 21	Superdome, New Orleans	Desmond Howard, WR/KR, Green Bay
XXXII	Jan. 25, 1998	Denver 31, Green Bay 24	Qualcomm Stadium, San Diego	Terrell Davis, RB, Denver

Halftime

Third Quarter

THE GAMES

9

THE UPSETS

By Curt Gowdy / NBC Broadcaster

I've done everything you can do in sports broadcasting, and my most memorable game is Super Bowl III.

At the time most everybody thought the AFL stunk. I had announced their games since 1962, and I did eight Jets games (in 1968), and I wasn't so sure.

When I got to Miami, I called (Jets coach) Weeb Ewbank up and asked if I could see him at practice. He finally let

HISTORIC FLIGHT Matt Snell's second-quarter touchdown run forged the first crack in the popular pregame opinion that the Jets and the AFL didn't stand a chance against the mighty Colts. The underdogs shocked the world, 16-7, at the Orange Bowl.

me in, and I saw an hour and a half of workouts. I didn't hear a word spoken.

The next day I watched the Colts in Fort Lauderdale. I saw guys laughing. I had a

beer with (running back) Tom Matte. I asked him what he thought, and he said he was

playing for the $15,000 winner's share and was building a play room for his home with

it. Bob Vogel, the lineman, said he'd go on an African safari with his winnings.

The morning of the game broke ominous and ugly. I was leaving for the Orange

Bowl when I ran into Howard Cosell, who was holding court. "Cowboy," he said, "the

FEARLESS FORECAST   Broadway Joe didn't shy away from the spotlight after the Jets won the AFL championship game. Once in Miami, Namath responded by directing the upset of the century by claiming MVP honors.

REVENGE FACTOR   Jets head coach Weeb Ewbank turned down a pregame invitation to a Colts victory party from Baltimore owner Carroll Rosenbloom. Ewbank had been fired as head coach by the Colts in 1962.

Colts are going to kill them. Bubba Smith is going to kill the Jets. But you're just going to be a shill for your league, aren't you, Cowboy?" I got into the car and told Al

DeRogatis, my NBC color man, "I feel like I'm ready to play the game. I'm mad!"

I won't say I was rooting for the Jets, but I wanted them to do well. At halftime

the Jets were ahead 7-0, and it was starting to sink in. By the fourth quarter it was

CAVALRY CHARGE The Jets and Broncos slew their Goliaths on the backs of punishing running warriors such as Matt Snell and Terrell Davis.

16-0, the outcome was no longer in doubt and it was getting dark. I told the audience they were witnessing one of the greatest upsets ever, one that would change the face of sports for all time. A lot of writers jumped on me for that, but it was true.

I'd say the guy who had the toughest job at Super Bowl III was Kyle Rote, who had to interview Shula in the Colts locker room after they lost. It was so quiet in there you could hear the shower dripping.

Curt Gowdy's six decades of sports broadcasting include play-by-play duties for NBC at six Super Bowls.

CLOSE CALLS

10

By Tony Veteri / Official

Every official works to get to the Super Bowl — it's the top of the list. You're graded after every game during the season, and the guys with the best marks are the ones who go. I worked four of them, and Super Bowl VII (Miami 14, Washington 7) was one of my best.

Most people probably remember the blocked kick that led to Garo

PURSUING PERFECTION

The only thing standing between Larry Csonka and the Dolphins' perfect season was a stubborn Redskins defensive effort in Super Bowl VII.

Yepremian's intercepted pass. When Mike Bass intercepted it and was running up the sidelines, someone pushed Yepremian out of the way and almost knocked me down. I had to jump over him, and I wanted to kill 'em (both). I remember saying to myself, "You little runt! Get out of my way!"

There was also the Dolphins' 47-yard touchdown pass from Bob Griese to Paul Warfield that I threw the flag on. Don Shula was on my back, saying that Warfield was never offsides — which was

KICKING AND SCREAMING The Cowboys' line of defense fell short of keeping Colts kicker Jim O'Brien out of Super Bowl legend. O'Brien's third field goal of the game, a 32-yard game winner with 5 seconds remaining, instantly gained recognition as the first dramatic finish among the first five Super Bowls.

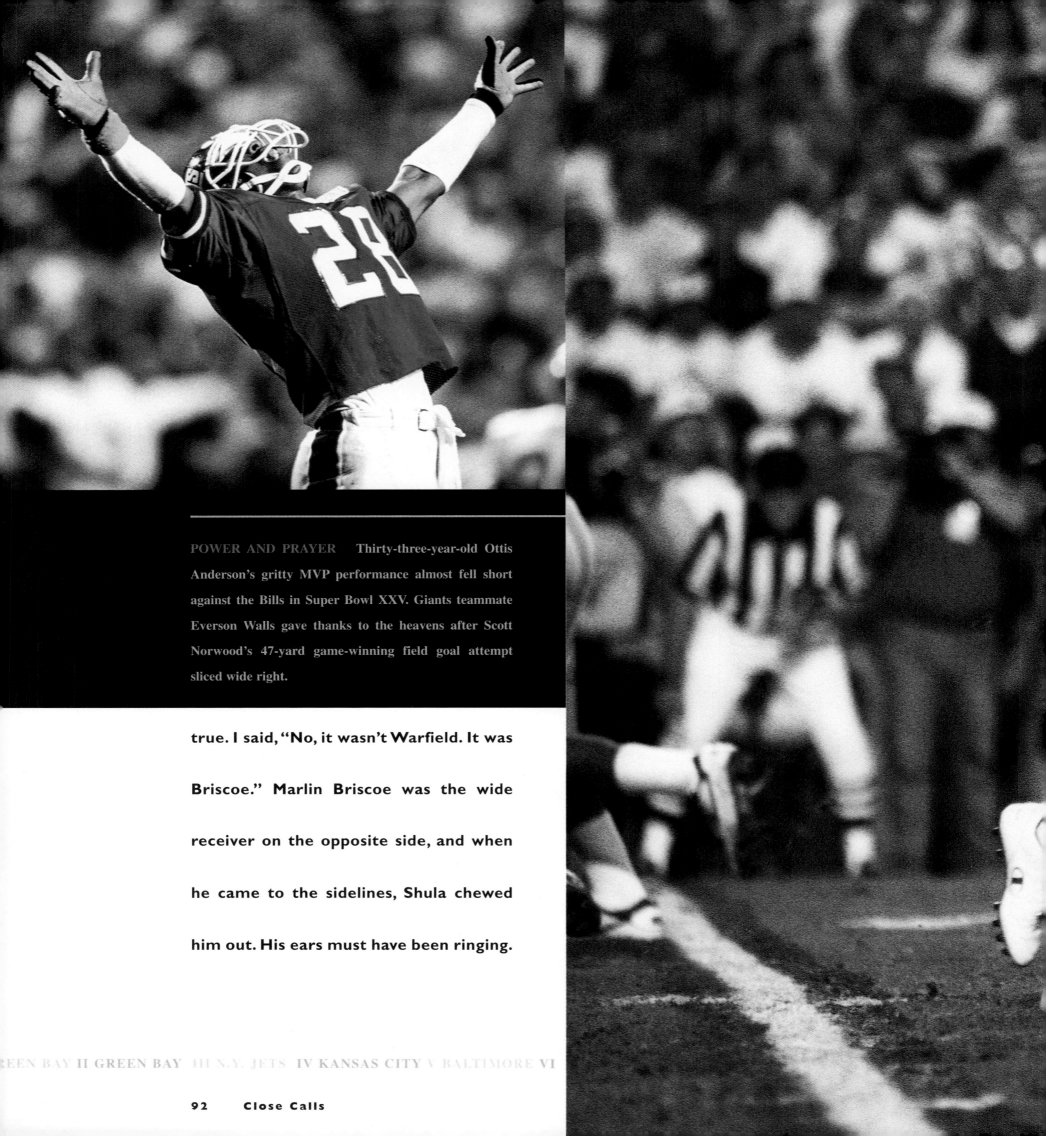

POWER AND PRAYER   Thirty-three-year-old Ottis Anderson's gritty MVP performance almost fell short against the Bills in Super Bowl XXV. Giants teammate Everson Walls gave thanks to the heavens after Scott Norwood's 47-yard game-winning field goal attempt sliced wide right.

true. I said, "No, it wasn't Warfield. It was Briscoe." Marlin Briscoe was the wide receiver on the opposite side, and when he came to the sidelines, Shula chewed him out. His ears must have been ringing.

"We've got 'em now."

— Bengals player near

end of XXIII

"Have you taken a look

at who's quarterbacking

the 49ers?"

— Bengals WR

Cris Collinsworth

The game itself was close and excit-

ing. That the Dolphins were undefeated

made it all the more memorable.

Tony Veteri served as a head linesman for the AFL and NFL from 1961 to 1983 and worked Super Bowls II, VII, XII and XV.

TIGER TAMERS The Bengals fell just short in their two Super Bowl tries against the 49ers. Joe Montana entered "The Drive" into the NFL lexicon in Super Bowl XXII and the 49ers' defense stuffed a comeback bid in Super Bowl XVI.

BLOWOUTS

By Vic Carucci / The Buffalo News Sportswriter

"Be objective! Don't let your emotions get the better of you! The task is the same whether they win or lose!"

I kept reciting those lines in my head as I sat in the Rose Bowl press box and watched the Dallas Cowboys mangle the Buffalo Bills in Super Bowl XXVII.

I knew I had to put aside the way I felt about the Bills' 52-17 loss, and calmly, professionally, tell my Buffalo News

A LITTLE HELP FROM HIS FRIENDS Bills quarterback Jim Kelly had to be helped off the field at one point during his team's 52-17 thrashing at the hands of the Dallas Cowboys. Kelly had attempted only seven passes before backup Frank Reich relieved him for the day.

readers how and why their team had

gone down to defeat in a **THIRD** consec-

utive **Super Bowl** and in such horrendous

fashion.

And that was exactly what I did.

But after filing my story and turning

off my laptop computer, I couldn't help

but feel a certain degree of emptiness.

It was something that almost every Western New Yorker experienced — the ones who traveled across the country to witness the carnage in person and the hundreds of thousands who suffered through it back home.

It is impossible to cover a team year-round for what then was 11 seasons and

HEAD OVER HEELS The always entertaining Jim McMahon led his Bears up and over the upstart New England Patriots in the 20th version of the big game by passing for 256 yards and running for two touchdowns. The Pats have never won a Super Bowl, and had some company in that matter until the Broncos finally broke through in Super Bowl XXXII. Still, Denver was all too familiar with the feeling of falling flat on their faces under the intense pressure of the NFL's championship battle.

not share at least a little of the hurt.

Even some of my colleagues felt compelled to offer condolences.

"Makes no difference to me," I said, pretending not to care. "Yeah," said one veteran scribe, "but it would still be nice for you to write about the Bills winning a Super Bowl just once."

I'm still waiting.

Sportswriter Vic Carucci has covered 18 Super Bowls, not to mention the Bills' four straight losses from 1991 to '94.

BRIDESMAIDS

12

By Adam Lingner / Ex-Bills Long-Snapper

I clearly remember our first Super Bowl: January 27, 1991, against the New York Giants. Late in the game we were behind, 20-19, and I was thinking, "Man, I could be involved in the play that wins the Super Bowl!"

Sure enough, with eight seconds remaining, our field goal unit assembled for a 47-yard attempt. I'd spent all week watching film of the Giants' field goal

WIDE RIGHT When Scott Norwood misfired that fateful night in 1991, little did the Buffalo Bills know that their first Super Bowl would be their only legitimate shot at a world title in the 20th century.

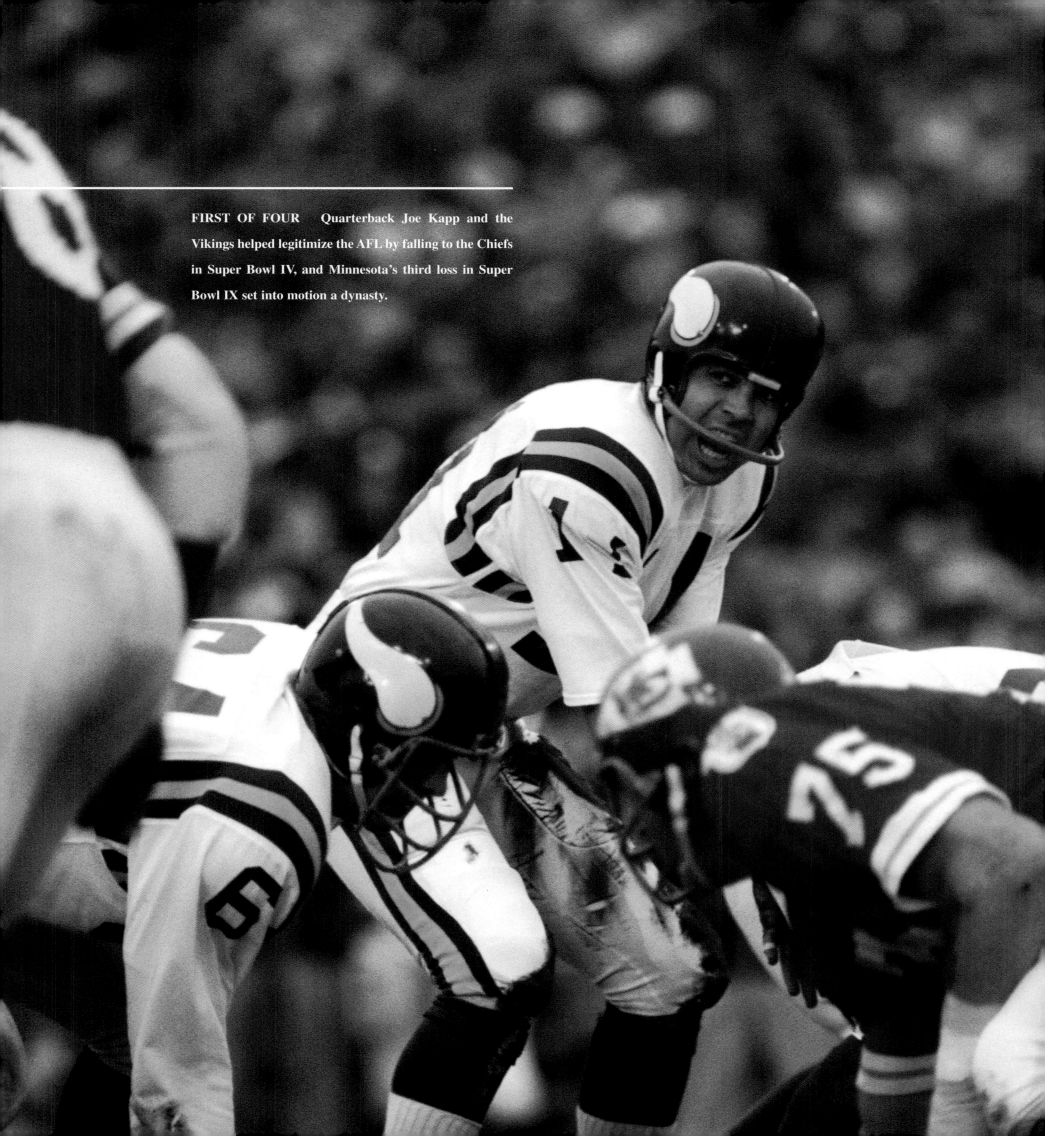

FIRST OF FOUR   Quarterback Joe Kapp and the Vikings helped legitimize the AFL by falling to the Chiefs in Super Bowl IV, and Minnesota's third loss in Super Bowl IX set into motion a dynasty.

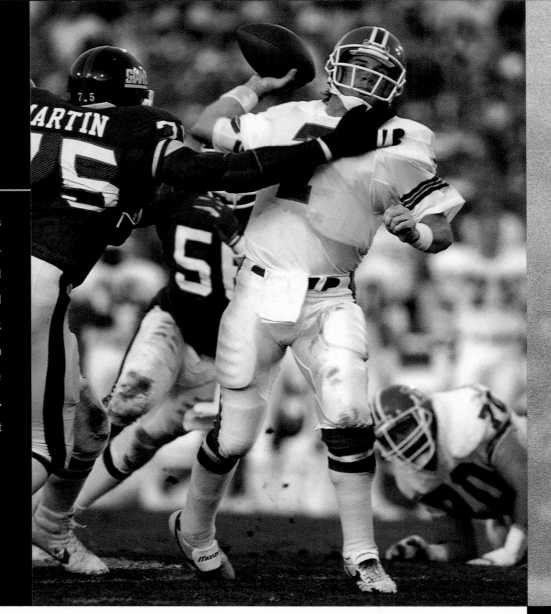

AGONY OF DEFEAT You don't have to tell the game's best quarterbacks that defense wins the Super Bowl. The N.Y. Giants' intimidating pass rush, spearheaded by George Martin and Lawrence Taylor, contained Denver's John Elway and shut down the running attack in the first of the Broncos' three defeats. Miami's Dan Marino and Cincinnati's Boomer Esiason saw their lone Super Sunday ruined by the 49ers' balanced defense. Dallas bent the Steel Curtain twice in the '70s but couldn't break the Steelers' hold on destiny.

rush, so I felt prepared as I bent over the ball.

Frank Reich's cadence: "Ready . . . set . . . SNAP."

As the Giants rushed and Scott Norwood's kick sailed overhead, I lost sight of the ball. Only the official's signal told me that the kick had missed and we had lost.

I was dejected for, oh, about 10 seconds. I couldn't feel awfully bad, because I'd known too many veteran players who'd never even been to the playoffs. I had to almost act like I was down so guys wouldn't think I didn't care.

"If I look back on my career and know that I worked hard and achieved a lot of personal goals, I'll be fulfilled. Because to win it all, you have to be lucky."

— Dan Marino

on winning the Big One

When we lost to Washington the next year, I didn't really feel bad about that. But I felt worse about the Giants game! It was the same when we lost to Dallas (in 1993), because I began to realize, "How many opportunities are we going to get?"

Losing four Super Bowls doesn't bother me. Winning would have been fun, but we had our chances because we were fighters. I'll never feel bad about that.

Adam Lingner, who played 13 NFL seasons, was the long-snapper in all four of the Bills' Super Bowl appearences.

Fourth
Quarter

THE PLAYERS

13

FLASHES IN THE PAN

By Desmond Howard / Super Bowl XXXI MVP

Because of the excitement of the event, which is unparalleled by any other game you ever play in, I don't think that I was ever in a zone in any game more than I was in that Super Bowl game. It all just started with the first return. The first return was a big one.

One play later we hit Andre (Rison) for a touchdown. Without a doubt, I had a feeling of invincibility that day. I mean I

HAPPY RETURNS Desmond Howard's 99-yard kick-off return for a touchdown in Super Bowl XXXI was the longest in postseason history. Better yet for Green Bay, Howard's MVP efforts answered a Patriots touchdown in the third quarter and clinched the Packers' triumph.

returned one later in the game that was

called back on some kind of bogus penal-

ty. I wasn't supposed to even return it.

But I was in that zone.

If I wind up being known more for

that one game than anything else, it's

hard to know how I will feel. You can't get

any higher than being crowned MVP of

the Super Bowl. Not in our profession.

You have MVPs of the league every year.

But to be MVP of the Super Bowl . . .

everyone's goal should be to at least go

to a Super Bowl and play in a Super Bowl.

OUT OF NOWHERE   An injury to starter George
Rogers thrust backup Timmy Smith into the Super Bowl
XXII spotlight. The rookie ripped the Broncos' defense
for a Super Bowl record 204 yards including a 58-yard
touchdown burst. Smith lasted just one more season with
the Redskins.

"The second quarter was easily the best quarter of football I've been around. Maybe now, they will look at Doug for something other than his color."

– head coach Joe Gibbs on his heroic quarterback

To be crowned the MVP of that game is just a blessing. It's something that only a few people can boast. Especially people who do what I do, which is return punts and kicks.

My whole goal now is to get back to the Super Bowl. Those who have been there know exactly what I am talking about. They want to taste it again. It's unbelievable.

Playing for his third team in three seasons, Desmond Howard became the first special teams player to be named Super Bowl MVP.

14

GOATS

By Garo Yepremian / Former Dolphins Kicker

During the warm-ups I realized I wasn't hitting the ball as high, and I was really line-driving it. I didn't feel good about the way I was kicking it. But here you are, a pro, and you can't really tell the coach, "I don't think I can do it today."

So, here it was, fourth down, a 42-yard field goal. I'd made a 54-yarder earlier in the year to beat Buffalo, 24-23, and

FALLEN STAR   Jackie Smith's reaction to an incompletion in the end zone during Super Bowl XIII remains etched in the minds of Cowboys fans as a missed opportunity. Roger Staubach still claims the pass was thrown behind Smith.

BAD IDEA That's what Miami's Garo Yepremian thought next in Super Bowl VII when cornerback Mike Bass intercepted Yepremian's feeble pass attempt and returned it for a touchdown.

FINE LINE BETWEEN WINNING AND LOSING Bills and Giants fans will always remember Scott Norwood going wide right on the final play of XXV. Vikings fans will always discuss what could have been.

a 51-yarder to beat Minnesota, 16-14. I usually was able to adjust to whatever was happening that day.

But it came time to kick the ball and the ball went just like it did in warm-ups. Earl Morrall — he was the holder — said, "Pick it up, pick it up." I said, "Why don't you?" But I pick it up and I'm thinking,

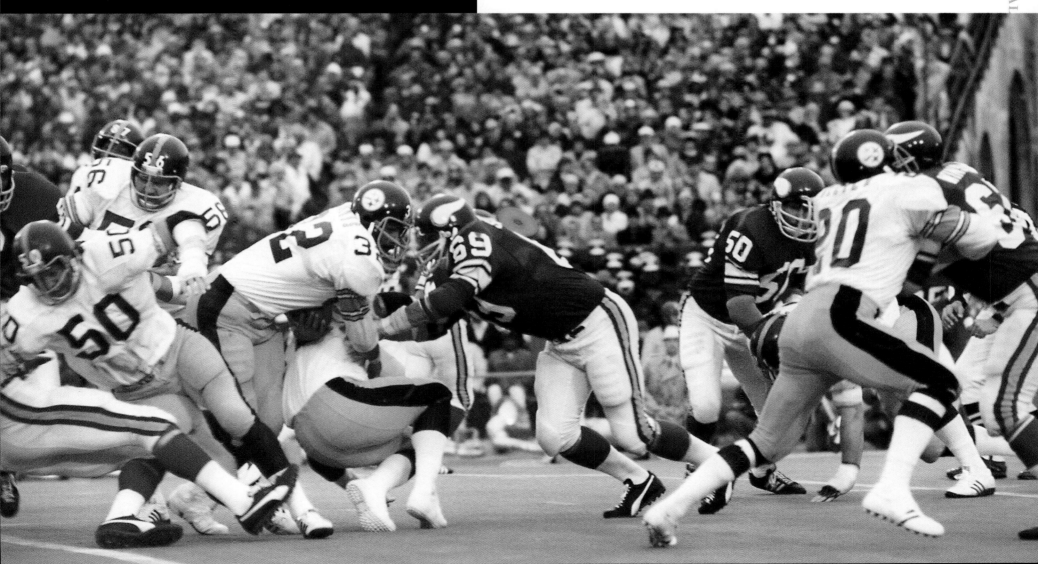

"What do I do now?"

I must have been watching a bunch of Terry Bradshaw films before that. But here comes (Redskins tackle) Bill Brundige at me with smoke coming out of his ears and mouth and I throw it. But I've got these normal-sized hands and it just slides off my hand, and (cornerback) Mike Bass grabs it.

The next thing I know Bass is running the other way and I'm looking for a place to hide from everybody else.

Coach (Don) Shula walked by and he glared, but all he said was, "You should have sat on the ball." That's all he said because he had to worry about the defense. Then (Miami offensive tackle) Norm Evans walked up to me and said, "Garo, don't worry. God will take care of you."

Fortunately, we won, so I didn't have to completely hide in the locker room. I

just told the reporters I made a mistake.

But I was miserable for two days. Then

somebody called and said, "We have a

banquet in Maine, and we'd like you to

come talk to us. We'll pay your expenses

and $2,000." I did 34 banquets and made

more money at banquets than I did dur-

ing the whole season.

Now, I make more in a year (on the

lecture circuit) than I did at any time in

my career. I've turned the biggest nega-

tive of my life into the biggest positive.

Garo Yepremian proved to be a much more capable kicker than passer during his stint with the Miami Dolphins, retiring as the team's leader in career points with 830 in 1978.

15

CHARACTERS

By Frank Luksa / Columnist

History remembers Super Bowl XIII for the name game that took place before the big game, when Thomas "Hollywood" Henderson had the first word but Terry Bradshaw got the last laugh.

Dallas vs. Pittsburgh was distinguished by the introduction of a spelling challenge to the Miami-based event. Henderson, the flamboyant Cowboys

DUMB MOVE Hollywood Henderson's bodacious blasts about Terry Bradshaw's IQ backfired in Super Bowl XIII when the sly Louisiana country boy passed for a record 318 yards and four TDs.

UNBEARABLE   Quarterback Jim McMahon looked
and sounded at times like he came from Pluto, but once
he, the Fridge and the Bears got rolling in Super Bowl
XX, the Patriots were flattened by the Super Bowl
Shuffle.

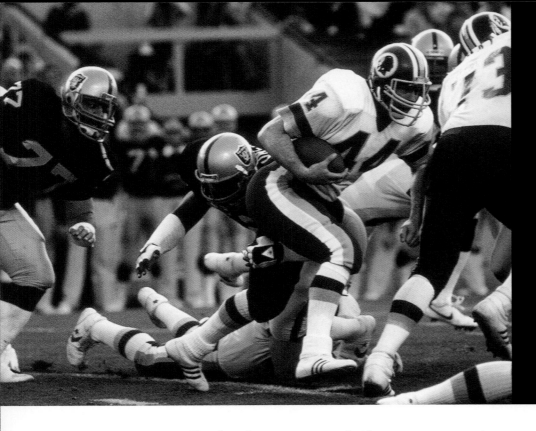

linebacker, captured the pregame stage with bombastic remarks aimed at the Steelers.

He said Jack Lambert's appearance offended "because he didn't have no teeth."

Nor did Hollywood think much of match-up opponent Randy Grossman, who'd replaced injured starter Bennie Cunningham:

"How much respect can you have for a reserve tight end? He's the guy who comes in when everyone else is dead."

Henderson fired his heaviest salvo at Bradshaw, playing off the quarterback's Lil' Abner persona. He sniffed and said, "Bradshaw couldn't spell 'cat' if you gave him the 'c' and the 'a'."

Bradshaw ignored the insult. Pittsburgh coach Chuck Noll defended his passer with a dry reply directed at Henderson. "Empty barrels make the

"The Jets will win on Sunday, I guarantee it."

— Joe Namath

"Maybe Namath represents the kind of athlete the coming generation wants. I hope not."

— Colts QB Earl Morrall, a day after The Prediction

NO DANCING Super Bowl XXIII lived up to its name — a 26-21 49ers victory. The only thing missing was the highly anticipated sight of the Bengals' Ickey Woods shuffling into the end zone.

most noise," Noll reminded.

I remember no one questioned Bradshaw's mental powers in the aftermath of the 35-31 victory by the Steelers. He threw four touchdown passes and audibled for the other, sending Franco Harris 22 yards to score on a draw play.

After the game, Bradshaw issued his version of a spelling challenge to Henderson. "How do you spell 'W-I-N?'"

Frank Luksa, a columnist for The Dallas Morning News, has worked 29 of the first 32 Super Bowls and ranks XIII in the top three for sheer thrills.

THE HEROES

16

By Lynn Swann / Ex-Steelers Wide Receiver

I had the fortune to play in four Super Bowl games, and they were all victories, so the memories are all good ones.

But probably the fondest memories were of Super Bowl X when (the Steelers) beat the Cowboys, 21-17. I think I caught four passes (for 161 yards) and scored a touchdown.

That was an important game for me because I was coming off an injury

STEALING THE SHOW Lynn Swann's clutch, acrobatic receptions in Super Bowl X overshadowed his great game in the rematch with Dallas in XIII: seven catches for 124 yards and an 18-yard, game-clinching scoring grab.

(a career-threatening concussion), and I was able to shake it off. I started the game and played a good game. One catch I get to see all the time is the one I made near midfield, the one where I caught the ball while I was falling down (over Cowboys cornerback Mark Washington). You look at it and think, "If I would have

DOUBLE VISION It was the Packers' defense seeing double – not Terrell Davis – when the Broncos' work-horse shook off a mild concussion in XXXII to rush for 93 yards and two touchdowns in the second half.

FREEZE FAME Great catches such as his famous juggling grab over Mark Washington in Super Bowl X helped earn four rings for Lynn Swann and the Pittsburgh dynasty.

STICKUM UP Sticky-fingered Fred Biletnikoff caught everything Ken Stabler threw his way – notably, a 48-yard reception to set up the game-icing TD – and the wily receiver carried off MVP honors in Super Bowl XI against Minnesota, the first of the Raiders' two world titles.

caught it the first time, it would not have been so dramatic."

That will probably always stick with me.

I think that game kind of defined my career. I didn't play as many years (nine, 1974-82) as some players, and that's probably the reason I'm not in the Hall of Fame.

All I can say is, "Gale Sayers." (The Bears' HOF running back played from 1965 to '71.)

ABC gave me an opportunity to become an expert commentator, and the offer was too good to turn down. I don't apologize for the length of time I played. Sure, I'd like to be in the Hall of Fame. Who wouldn't want to be in? But I have four Super Bowls I can look back on.

Lynn Swann, a three-time Pro Bowl receiver for Pittsburgh, ranks behind only Jerry Rice in career Super Bowl receiving yards (364).

CONTRIBUTORS

Writers

Vernon Biever Team photographer for the Packers, recounted his own experiences of the Green Bay teams of the 1960s for Chapter 5.

Vic Carucci NFL beat writer for The Buffalo News, recounted his own experience of Super Bowl XXVII for Chapter 11.

Dwight Chapin A columnist for the San Francisco Examiner, interviewed Randy Cross for Chapter 7.

Jason Cole NFL beat writer for the Fort Lauderdale Sun-Sentinel, interviewed Jimmy Johnson for Chapter 8 and Garo Yepremian for Chapter 14.

Gerry Dulac A columnist for the Pittsburgh Post-Gazette, interviewed Jack Ham for Chapter 6 and Lynn Swann for Chapter 16.

John Hickey A sportswriter for the Oakland Tribune, interviewed Desmond Howard for Chapter 13.

Todd Korth Editor of The Packer Report, interviewed Brett Favre for the Foreword.

Clay Latimer NFL beat writer for The Rocky Mountain News, interviewed Pat Bowlen for Chapter 3.

Frank Luksa A columnist for The Dallas Morning News, recounted his own experience of Super Bowl XIII for Chapter 15.

Tim O'Shei The editor of the Buffalo Bills fan magazine Shout, interviewed Tony Veteri for Chapter 10 and Adam Lingner for Chapter 12.

Fritz Quindt A columnist for the San Diego Union Tribune, interviewed Dick Enberg, Michael T. Fiur, Dan Fouts and Curt Gowdy for Chapters 1, 2, 4 and 9, respectively.

Photographers

Vernon J. Biever contributed a majority of the photos for this book.

Other Contributors

James V. Biever
John E. Biever / Sports Illustrated
Tom DiPace
Malcolm Emmons / NFL Photos
Bill Frakes / Sports Illustrated
John Iacono / Sports Illustrated
Walter Iooss / Sports Illustrated

Walter Iooss, Jr. / Sports Illustrated
Heinz Kluetmeier / NFL Photos
Neil Leifer / Sports Illustrated
Richard Mackson / NFL Photos
Ronald C. Modra / Sports Illustrated
Richard Pilling / NFL Photos
George Rose / NFL Photos
Herb Scharfman / Sports Illustrated
Chuck Solomon / Sports Illustrated
Al Tielemans / Sports Illustrated
Tony Tomsic / Sports Illustrated
Jerry Wachter / Sports Illustrated